Pumas

Victoria Blakemore

© 2018 Victoria Blakemore

All rights reserved. This book or parts thereof may not be reproduced in any form, stored in any retrieval system, or transmitted in any form by any means—electronic, mechanical, photocopy, recording, or otherwise—without prior written permission of the publisher, except as provided by United States of America copyright law. For permission requests, write to the publisher, at "Attention: Permissions Coordinator," at the address below.

vblakemore.author@gmail.com

Copyright info/picture credits

Cover, Baranov/AdobeStock; Page 3, Kaz/Pixabay; Page 5, strichpunkt/Pixabay; Page 7, hkuchera/AdobeStock; Page 9, Annamaria/Adobestock; Pages 10-11, Pexels/Pixabay; Page 13, 3031830/Pixabay; Page 15, Dennis Donohue/AdobeStock; Page 17, mikaelmales/AdobeStock; Page 19, Dennis Donohue/AdobeStock; Page 21, skeeze/Pixabay; Page 23; PublicDomainPictures/Pixabay; Page 25, photosbykathys/Twenty20; Page 27, geoffkuchera/AdobeStock; Page 29, skeeze/Pixabay; Page 31, hecke71/AdobeStock; Page 33, Baranov/AdobeStock

Table of Contents

What are Pumas?	2
Size	4
Physical Characteristics	6
Habitat	8
Range	10
Diet	12
Communication	16
Movement	18
Puma Cubs	20
Puma Life	22
Florida Panthers	24
Population	26
Pumas in Danger	28
Helping Pumas	30
Glossary	34

What Are Pumas?

Pumas are large mammals. They are members of the small cat family. Other small cats include servals and lynxes.

Pumas have different names in different places. They are called mountain lions, cougars, or panthers depending on where they are.

Pumas are usually tan, golden brown, and beige in color.

Size

Pumas can grow to be between three and five feet long. Their tail can be two or three feet long.

When they are fully grown, pumas weigh between about seventy and one hundred sixty pounds.

Male pumas are usually much larger than female pumas.

Physical Characteristics

Pumas that live in colder areas have a thick coat of fur. It helps them to stay warm.

Their **hind** legs are longer than their front legs. They are also very strong. This allows pumas to move quickly and leap over long distances.

Pumas have a long, thick tail.

Their tail helps them to balance when they are climbing trees.

Habitat

Pumas have adapted to live in many different habitats. They are found in forests, deserts, grasslands, mountains, and parts of the rainforest.

Many pumas live in places with lots of rocky areas, grasses, and bushes. This allows them to **stalk** their prey.

Range

Pumas are found on the continents of North and South America.

They are often seen in countries like Canada, Brazil, Peru, and the United States.

Diet

Pumas are **carnivores**. They eat only meat.

Their diet is made up of deer, squirrels, raccoons, hares, pigs, moose, and armadillos. In South America, they also feed on capybaras.

Pumas have very good eyesight. They are able to easily spot prey by watching for movement.

When hunting, pumas stay hidden until prey comes near. When it is close enough, the puma pounces and knocks down the prey.

They have also been known to chase prey if needed. Their size and speed makes it easy for them to catch their prey.

Pumas are able to leap long distances to catch their prey. They can leap as far as twenty feet.

Communication

Pumas use mainly sound and scent to communicate with each other. They are known for making a high-pitched scream.

They use scent markings to send messages to other pumas. They also purr, mew, yowl, hiss, and squeak.

Pumas cannot roar, but they can snarl and scream. They also pull their ears back when they are angry.

Movement

Pumas are able to move very quickly. They have been known to run at speeds up to fifty miles per hour in a fast sprint.

They are also good at swimming. However, they are rarely seen in the water. They seem to prefer being on land.

Pumas are good at climbing trees. This helps them to stay safe from larger predators such as bears or jaguars.

Puma Cubs

Pumas have a **litter** of between one and six babies. Their babies are called cubs.

Mother pumas are very **protective** of their cubs. They keep them safe from predators like bears. They also teach their cubs how to hunt.

Cubs are born with dark spots.

Their spots work as **camouflage**.

They fade after about six months.

Puma Life

Pumas are usually **solitary** animals. They spend most of their time alone.

They are **crepuscular**, which means that they are most active at dawn and dusk. The low light at those times helps them to sneak up on their prey.

Pumas do not have a den they stay in. They move around often and sleep in different places.

Florida Panthers

Although they are called panthers, Florida panthers are actually a kind of puma. They are one of the smallest and **rarest** pumas.

They can be **identified** by their crooked tail and a patch of fur on their back that grows in a different direction.

The Florida panther is **critically endangered**. There are very few left in the wild.

Population

Most pumas are not **endangered**, but it is thought that their populations are **declining**.

It can be hard for researchers to know exactly how many pumas there are. They have large **ranges** and can be hard to find.

In the wild, pumas often live between eight and thirteen years. Some pumas may live as long as twenty years.

Pumas in Danger

Pumas are facing many threats. In some places, they are hunted for their meat and skin. They are also killed by people who think they are pests.

Their habitats are being destroyed for buildings, roads, and farming.

In some areas, people hunt animals that are prey for pumas. This can make it hard for them to find food.

Helping Pumas

In some places, special protected areas have been set up. They provide animals like pumas with safe habitats to live in.

In many countries, there are laws that protect pumas. It is **illegal** to kill them.

Some groups focus on research and education. They want to learn more about pumas so they can help them.

They also teach people about pumas. They hope that people will want to help pumas if they know more about them.

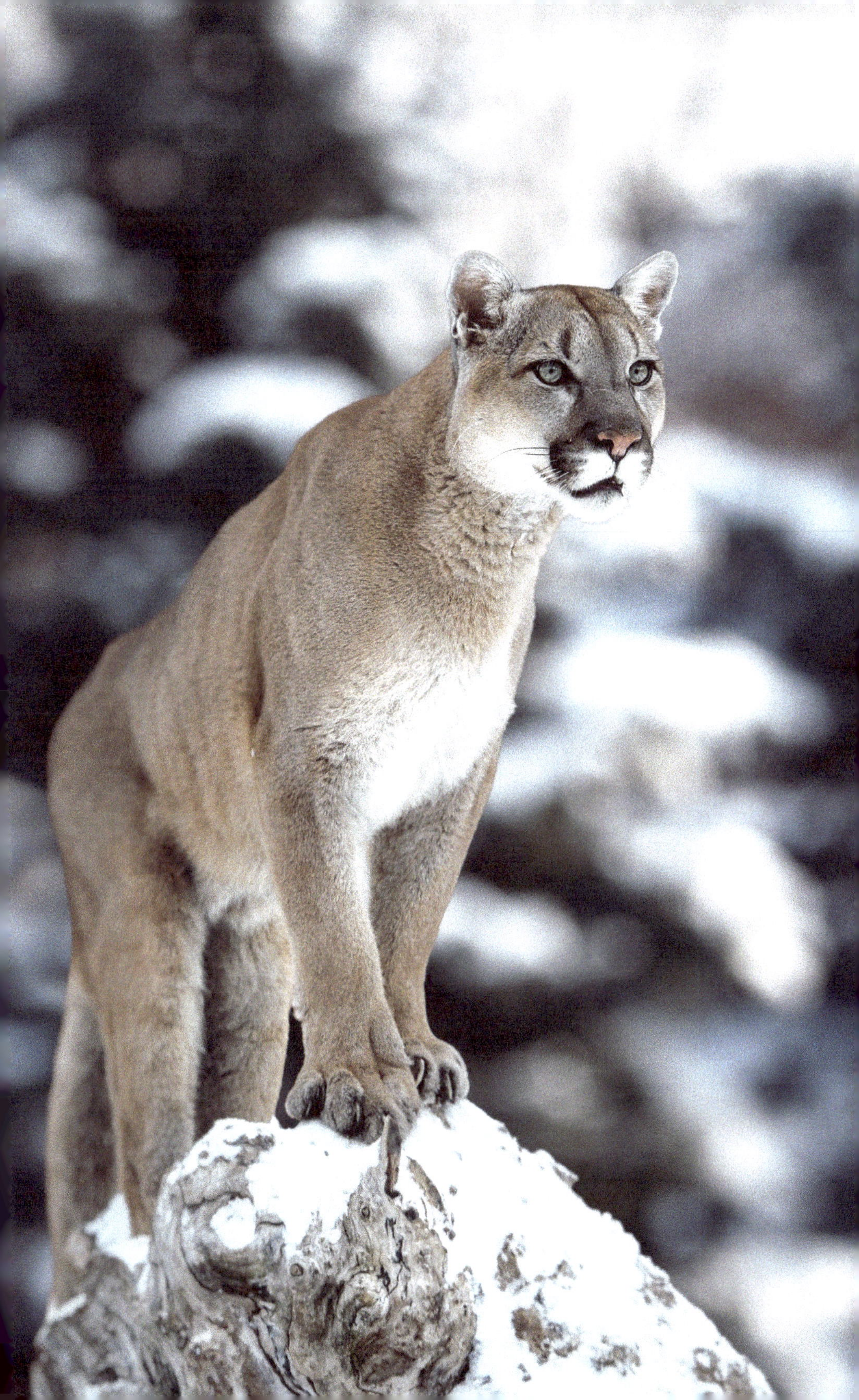

Glossary

Camouflage: using color to blend in to the surroundings

Carnivore: an animal that eats only meat

Crepuscular: active at dawn and dusk

Critically Endangered: very close to being extinct

Declining: getting smaller

Endangered: at risk of becoming extinct

Hind: back

Identify: to figure out what something is

Illegal: against the law

Litter: a group of animals born at the same time

Protective: taking care of, watchful over

Ranges: home territories

Rarest: most uncommon

Solitary: preferring to be alone

Stalk: when an animal follows prey carefully

About the Author

Victoria Blakemore is a first grade teacher in Southwest Florida with a passion for reading.

You can visit her at

www.elementaryexplorers.com

Also in This Series

Gray Wolves	Sloths	Flamingos	Camels	Koalas	Honey Bees	Pandas	
Pangolins	White-Tailed Deer	Orcas	Giraffes	Corn	Meerkats	Echidnas	
Walruses	Raccoons	Bald Eagles	Apples	Arctic Foxes	Red Pandas	Cassowaries	
Tigers	Ladybugs	Moose	Beluga Whales	Leopards	Elephants	Jellyfish	
Binturongs	Lions	Dolphins	Reindeer	Hammerhead Sharks	Hippos	Pumpkins	
Peafowl	Chameleons	Florida Panthers	Aye-Ayes	Black Bears	Cheetahs	Manatees	
Gingerbread	Polar Bears	Hot Chocolate	Orangutans	Coyotes	Marshmallows	Strawberries	

Also in This Series

Aardvarks, Mako Sharks, Alligators, Frogs, Hedgehogs, Brown Bears, Bongos, Sea Turtles, Quokkas, Muskrats, Zebras, Red Foxes, Ring-Tailed Lemurs, Platypuses, Anteaters, Kangaroos, Rhinos, Jaguars, Wombats, Capybaras, Gorillas, Cats, Skunks, Butterflies, Dingoes, Snow Leopards, African Wild Dogs, Penguins, Whale Sharks, Wolverines, Warthogs, Caracals, Badgers, Seals, Hummingbirds, Pikas, Humpback Whales, Pumas, Lemonade, Llamas, Tulips, Ostriches, Sunflowers, Fennec Foxes

CPSIA information can be obtained
at www.ICGtesting.com
Printed in the USA
LVHW071528060721
692000LV00005B/547

Children's 599.7524
Blakemore, Victoria
Pumas

08/20/21